THE EXPLOITATION OF SPACE

Tim Furniss

World Issues

The Arms Trade
Cities in Crisis
Endangered Wildlife
The Energy Crisis
The Environment
The Exploitation of Space
Food or Famine?
Human Rights
The International Debt Crisis
The International Drugs Trade
International Terrorism
Nuclear Power
Nuclear Weapons
Population Growth
Refugees
Sport and Politics
Threatened Cultures
World Health

Cover: The launch of the space shuttle *Discovery* in 1985.
Frontispiece: An astronaut from the space shuttle *Discovery* repairing a stranded satellite.

Editor: Mike Hirst
Series Designer: David Armitage

First published in 1989 by
Wayland (Publishers) Ltd.
61 Western Road, Hove
East Sussex, BN3 1JD, England

British Library Cataloguing in Publication Data
Furniss, Tim
The exploitation of space. – (World Issues)
1. Outer space – For schools
I. Title II. Series
523

ISBN 1–85210–608–5

Phototypeset by Kalligraphics Ltd., Horley, Surrey
Printed and bound in Italy by Sagdos S.p.A., Milan

Contents

1. Introduction 6

2. Space, satellites and orbits 8

3. The benefits of space research 13

4. The costs of space research 17

5. The growing problem of space debris 28

6. The militarization of space 33

7. Space – the final frontier? 43

Glossary 46

Books to read 47

Index 48

1 Introduction

The Space Age began on 4 October 1957, when for the first time, a satellite was sent into an orbit around the Earth. The satellite, which was called Sputnik 1 and belonged to the Soviet Union, opened an era of space exploration. This era of space exploration reached its peak in the late 1960s and early 1970s; men walked on the Moon for the first time and unmanned spacecraft travelled even further, exploring the planets of our solar system.

Space probes still explore other planets today; but the nations that launch spacecraft now tend to concentrate their efforts on developing satellites and finding ways of using space to benefit people on the Earth.

Making use of Space

Satellites have made it easier to forecast the weather and have improved our knowledge of the Earth's environment. Remote-sensing satellites, studying the Earth from space, have surveyed the planet's surface in great detail and on a scale not possible before. These remote-sensing satellites have monitored pollution and found new sources of minerals. They have also drawn maps of remote parts of the world that have not been charted before.

Most important of all, satellites have revolutionized long-distance communications. They have made it much easier to transmit telephone, radio and television signals right around the world. Probably the current revolution in telecommunications is as important to people in the late twentieth century as the Industrial Revolution was to parts of Europe during the nineteenth century.

So today, we no longer just explore space, but also exploit it. The word exploitation can be used to suggest either a good or a bad action. Space can be exploited to benefit humankind. Yet space is also exploited in other, more harmful ways. For example, present-day society is creating so much debris in space that future generations may not be able to enter it. Moreover, the United States and Soviet Union are developing new weapons which are making space into a battleground; and, although many people believe that these weapons maintain peace and the balance of power, the technology which they employ could easily be misused.

Another major problem is the high cost of space programmes. Space stations, like the USA's planned Freedom *space station*, cost

An antenna dish in West Germany which can receive radio signals which have been sent out by satellites.

An artist's impression of what a future military satellite might look like when positioned in orbit above the Earth.

hundreds of millions of dollars to build. Satellites are also very expensive to launch. The ideal solution to these high costs would be a spacecraft which, unlike today's rockets, could be used over and over again. Even the US space shuttle is only partly reusable, and much more money must be spent on research before the United States can develop a completely reusable spacecraft. Satellites are still launched for short-term commercial gain today without anything being done about reducing the enormous cost of space transportation.

The exploitation of space can bring enormous benefits to people. Yet many problems are still to be solved if the people of the world are to use outer space safely and wisely.

2 Space, satellites and orbits

The Earth and its atmosphere

The planet Earth is surrounded by a layer of gases, called the atmosphere. The lower atmosphere is made up mainly of oxygen and nitrogen. These gases are vitally important. They are the air we breathe and without them there would be no life on Earth.

As it extends upwards from the Earth's surface, the atmosphere changes. The air becomes thinner or less dense. This is the reason that climbers who go up very high mountains need oxygen masks to help them breathe properly. In the upper atmosphere there are also layers of other, special, gases which protect the Earth. The most important of these layers is the ozone layer, which shields life on Earth from radiation from the Sun.

The Earth's atmosphere ends altogether at a height of approximately 350 km. Beyond the atmosphere lies space.

What is space?

Space is completely empty, what scientists call a vacuum. There are no gases and no normal atmosphere. The sky is black all around.

Unlike the Earth's surface, which is shielded by the atmosphere, everything in space is exposed to a harsh environment. There is no protection from meteorites and radiation from the Sun and other stars. Harsh sunlight causes temperatures of over 110° celcius and in those parts of space where sunlight is blocked out, there is intense cold.

The space closest to the Earth forms part of our solar system. Within the solar system are the Earth and eight other planets, all of which move around the Sun. Beyond Pluto, the remotest planet, lies deep space, with its millions of distant stars and their own solar systems.

Opposite *A diagram showing the layers of the Earth's atmosphere.*

Below *Intelsat 5, one of the most up-to-date communications satellites.*

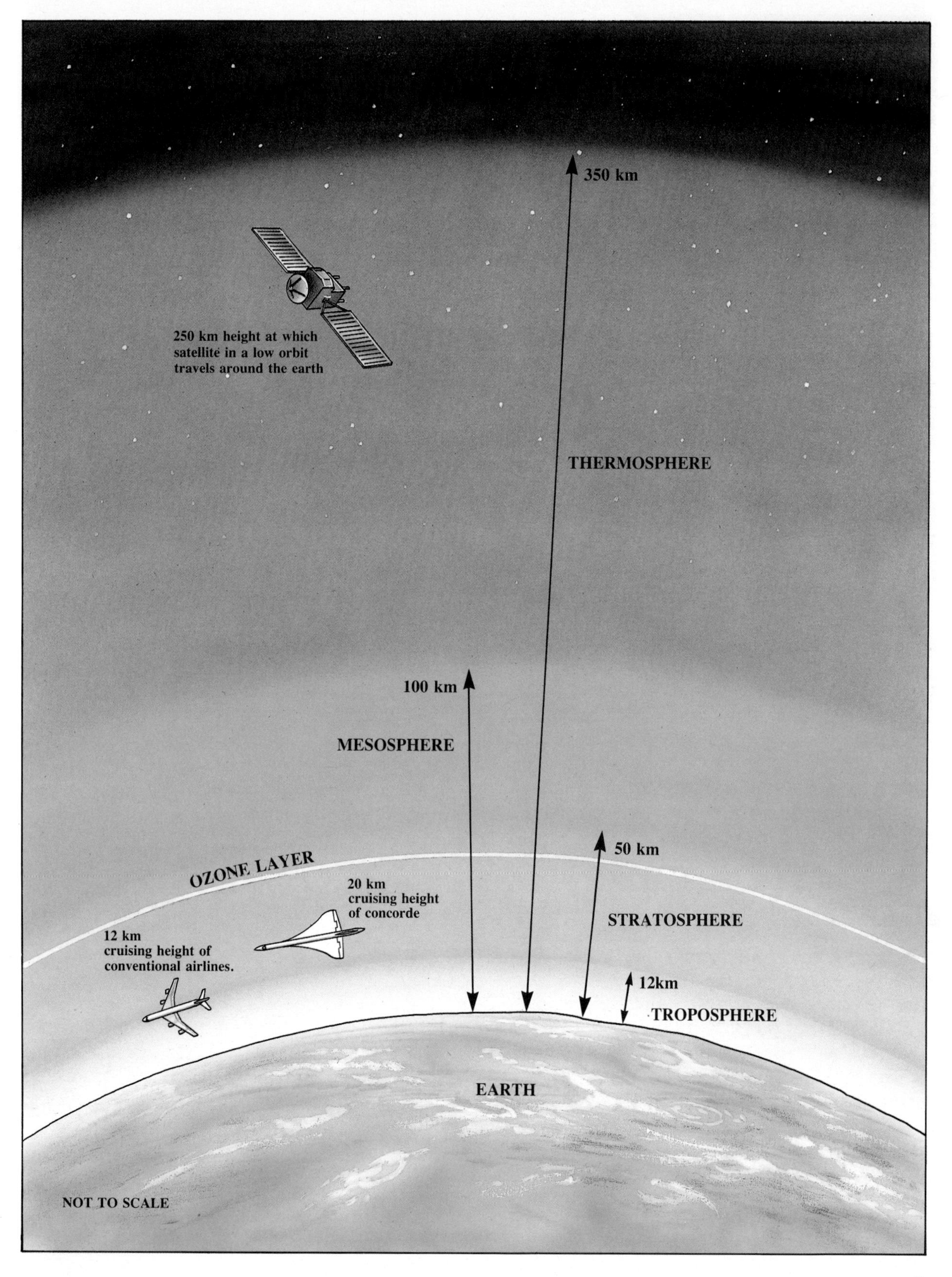
350 km
250 km height at which
satellite in a low orbit
travels around the earth
THERMOSPHERE
100 km
MESOSPHERE
50 km
OZONE LAYER
20 km
cruising height
of concorde
STRATOSPHERE
12 km
cruising height of
conventional airlines.
12km
TROPOSPHERE
EARTH
NOT TO SCALE

The re-entry module of the Apollo 11 spacecraft. Part of the gold-coloured protective heatshield burnt away when the module re-entered the Earth's atmosphere.

Satellites

The word 'satellite' was originally used to describe a planet which moves around, or orbits, another larger planet or star. The Moon is the natural satellite of the Earth. The Earth itself is a satellite of the Sun.

Today, however, the word satellite is usually used to describe a spacecraft, built by humans and specially launched into space to orbit the planet Earth.

Satellites are sent into orbit around the Earth by rockets which travel at very high speeds. These speeds are so great that when the satellite is released from the rocket, it is travelling fast enough to overcome the pull of the Earth's gravity. However, although the satellite is moving quickly enough not to be pulled back to Earth, it does not travel so fast as to be able to escape the pull of the Earth's gravity completely. Instead of speeding into deep space, it becomes 'trapped' in a continuous arc or orbit around the Earth.

If a satellite is close to the Earth, in a low orbit, it must travel very fast to avoid being pulled back to Earth by the force of gravity. For example, a satellite in an orbit about 250 km high must travel at a speed of 28,800 kph. At this speed, it will go around the Earth once every 90 minutes. Further away from the Earth, the pull of gravity becomes less strong, and satellites that are in higher orbits do not need to travel so fast.

Although the Earth's atmosphere becomes thinner at high altitudes, it still extends many kilometres above sea level. Even at a height of 250 km, there is a very small amount of air. Satellites in a low orbit are gradually slowed down because of this atmosphere. As they slow down, they are unable to resist the pull of the Earth's gravity, and fall back down to Earth. Usually, satellites re-entering the Earth's atmosphere are travelling so fast that they burn up completely. However, sometimes parts of a satellite can survive re-entry.

Some satellites carry people or special instruments that need to be brought back to the Earth safely. These satellites are fitted with heatshields to stop them from burning up. The American space shuttle has special, heat resistant tiles that protect it. The Russian Soyuz spacecraft has a heatshield that actually burns away during re-entry. The crew inside the space capsule are protected because the heat never reaches them.

Orbits

There are many different types of orbit. They differ in height above the Earth's surface, from as low as 250 km to over 36,000 km. They also differ in shape; some are circular, whilst others, called eccentric orbits, are oval shaped.

A satellite which is designed to survey the Earth will typically have what is called a low polar orbit. It will fly at a height of around 250 km, in a circle over the North and South Poles, crossing the Equator at an angle of 90°.

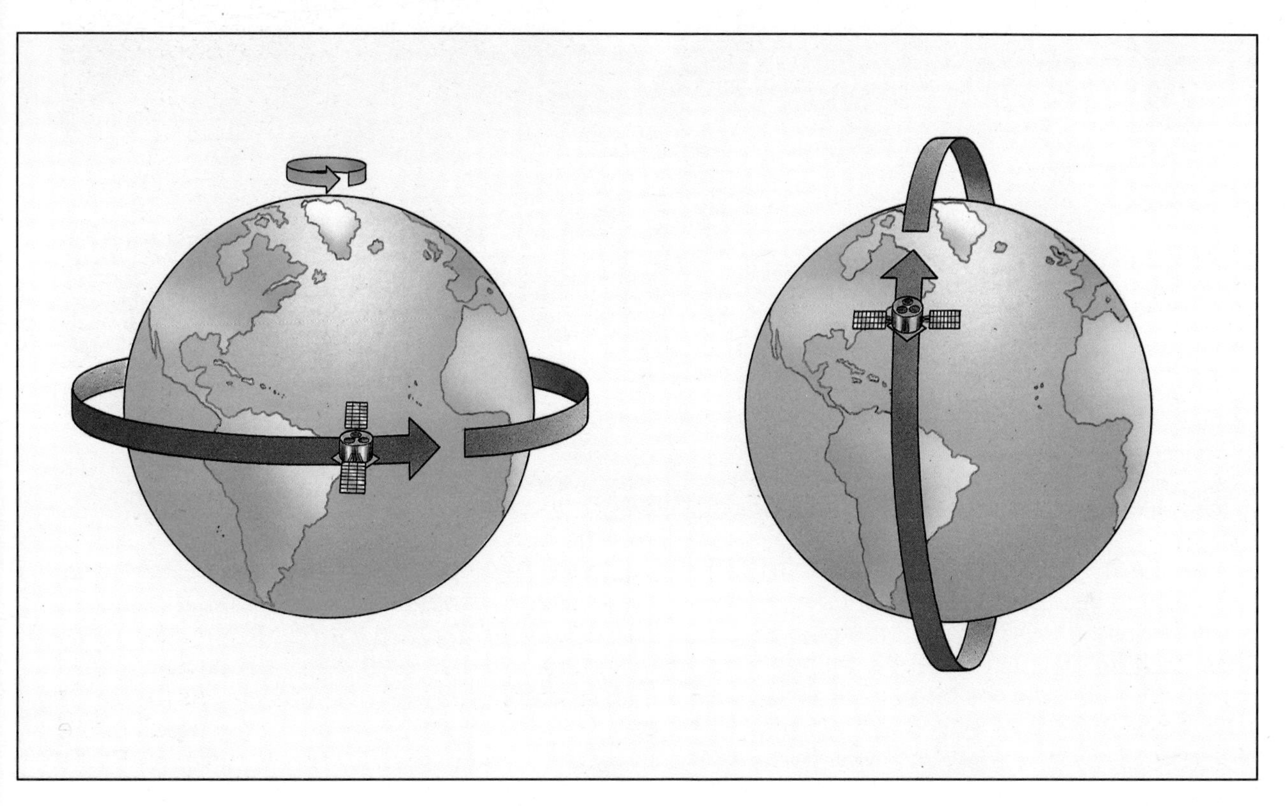

Above *A diagram showing satellites in low polar orbit (right) and geostationary orbit (left). The Earth rotates from left to right.*

Below *A diagram showing a group of navigational satellites in orbits at an angle of 60° to the Equator.*

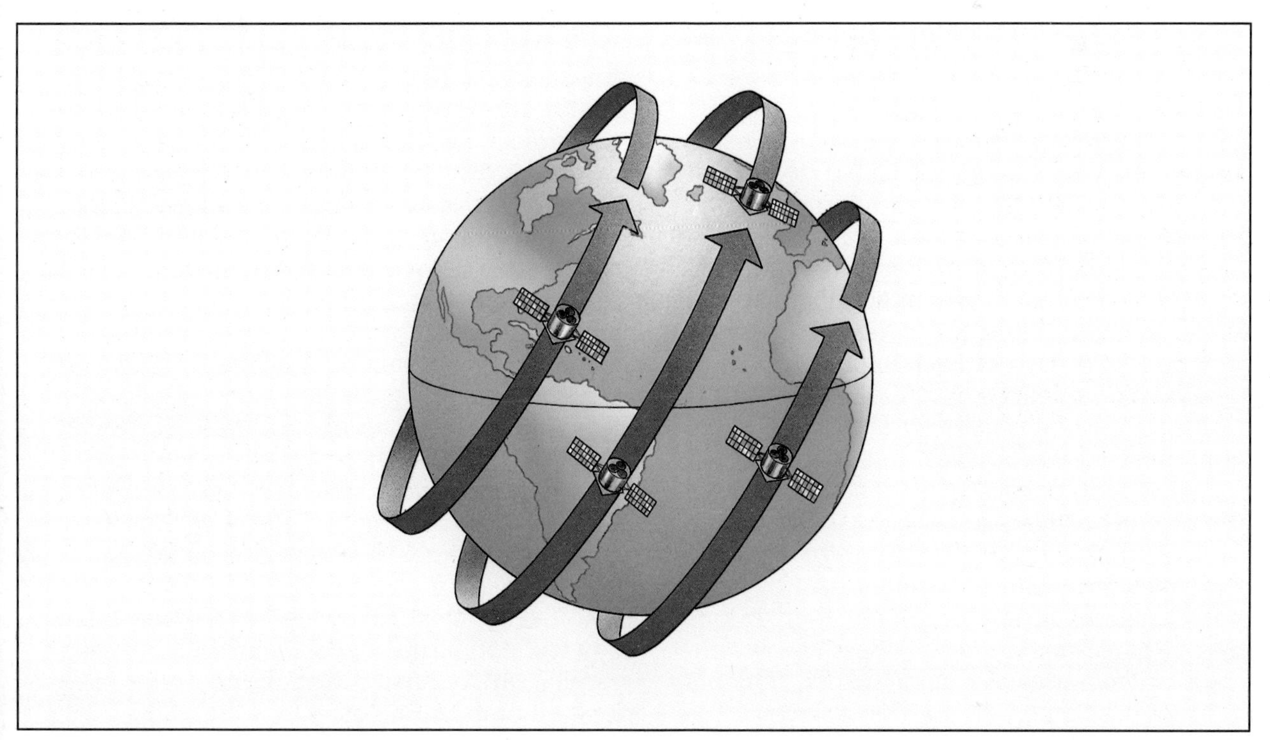

As the Earth rotates beneath it, the satellite flies around the Earth about 17 times a day, passing close to every part of the planet's surface. Such an orbit is ideal for satellites which monitor the weather, or for spy satellites.

The best-known satellites are communications satellites. They allow us to watch live television pictures of events happening on the other side of the world. They relay telephone calls, computer data and other information.

Communications satellites go into very high circular orbits, flying at 36,000 km above the Earth's surface, right around the Equator. In this orbit, satellites travel at the same speed as the Earth goes round, and so they appear to 'hover' directly above one place on the Earth's surface. This kind of orbit is called geo-stationary. Three satellites placed apart in such a geostationary orbit allow the transmission of television signals right around the world, the satellites acting as television aerials in space. At the moment, there are over one hundred such geostationary satellites in orbit.

Navigation satellites have a different kind of orbit again. They usually fly about 19,000 km high, crossing the Equator at an angle of 60°. For navigation purposes, a group of satellites are placed in this orbit in rings around the Earth. A transmitter on the surface of the Earth can make radio contact with at least three of these satellites at any one time. By fixing its position in relation to the three satellites, a vehicle fitted with special equipment can work out its exact position on the Earth's surface.

During the Apollo space project, American astronauts planted the Stars and Stripes, the United States flag, on the Moon; yet the Apollo landing did not give the United States any territorial rights over the Moon.

Who owns space?

Although there is so much activity in space, no single, worldwide organization owns or controls space. Each nation is responsible for the spacecraft that it sends into space. When American astronauts first landed on the Moon in 1969, they planted the United States flag on the surface. Yet the United States does not now own the Moon.

The United Nations, an organization with representatives from many countries of the world, tries to watch over space activities, to make sure that space is not misused. The success of this role depends on the honesty of the member countries. For example, all member countries must announce any satellite launch along with details of the satellite and its orbit. However, both the United States and the Soviet Union have tried to launch satellites secretly. These satellites were only discovered once they were in orbit by special tracking posts on the Earth, called surveillance stations.

All nations that use space have agreed that they will not misuse it, contaminate it or make war in it. As we shall see, many countries have done all of these things!

3
The benefits of space research

Telstar, the first satellite to transmit live television pictures across the Atlantic.

Why bother to launch spacecraft at all? Sometimes this question is easy to answer. Some of the benefits of space research affect everyone's lives. Other benefits are much less obvious and are not so widely understood.

The communications revolution

Probably the greatest single benefit from space research is the advance in long-distance communications. On July 10, 1962, a Thor Delta rocket lifted off into the night sky above Cape Canaveral in Florida. It launched a small, white satellite, called Telstar, which began a revolution in telephone and television communications. Within hours of Telstar reaching orbit, television viewers in Europe were able, for the first time, to see live television from the United States. The television signals were sent from a special station in the United States and beamed up to Telstar as it passed over the Atlantic Ocean. The satellite then retransmitted them towards another station in Europe, which fed the pictures to European television stations. Telstar caused great excitement and was a perfect example of how space could be used to directly benefit people.

A new satellite, called Syncom, followed Telstar. Syncom was the first satellite to go into geostationary orbit. Appearing to hover above one spot, it could receive and redirect television pictures for 24 hours a day. Another satellite, nicknamed Early Bird, followed in 1965. Eventually a fleet of satellites entered geostationary orbit. Today, they are used regularly to transmit television pictures, telephone calls and computer data around the world.

The most recent communications satellites are improving communications even further. The new Intelsat VI satellite is the size of a house. It can transmit four television broadcasts and 30,000 telephone calls all at the same time. Direct broadcasting satellites will be able to transmit even more television channels.

Some people have strong reservations about satellite broadcasting. They are worried that governments will have little control over what is shown on international satellite television, and fear that programmes will be of poor quality. However, satellite communications have also brought many unarguable benefits.

Satellites have not only reduced costs, but have also made it much easier to communicate with distant parts of the world. They have brought the world closer together and have created what some people call 'the global village.' Because people can see direct television pictures of what is happening in other parts of the world, they feel more concerned about their fellow humans who are suffering from wars or natural disasters such as earthquakes. Cheaper long-distance telephone calls make it easier for members of a family living in different countries to keep in touch.

Search and rescue, weather and remote-sensing satellites

The benefits of weather satellites are also felt in everyday life and most television weather forecasts now show pictures from weather satellites. A network of satellites in geostationary and polar orbits provide a constant watch on the world's weather. Hurricanes or typhoons can be spotted early and their paths worked out. Warnings can be issued and people evacuated. Property can be protected and the economies of the affected countries can be saved.

Satellites also control a search and rescue service, which has saved hundreds of lives. Distress signals can be sent out from boats, planes and trucks in trouble, usually in extremely remote parts of the world where help is not easily to hand. The signals are picked up by United States and Soviet satellites. These signals are then transmitted to special ground stations which can fix the position of the person in distress, and send out rescue teams. The same satellites have also been used by zoologists. United States scientists have studied the behaviour of American moose, by tracking their movements. Special collars attached to the animals' necks transmitted signals which were picked up by satellites.

Remote-sensing satellites also have many uses. The first of these satellites, the US Earth Resources Technology Satellite, was launched in 1972. More recently, the US company Eosat has put Landsat remote-sensing satellites into orbit. Many different people benefit from the information provided by these satellites. Farmers can tell if their crops are diseased, and when they are ready for harvest. Remote parts of the world can be mapped. Geologists can find new sources of minerals.

Perhaps most important of all, remote-sensing satellites have helped scientists to monitor pollution. In particular, satellites have shown us how we are polluting the atmosphere. Carbon dioxide levels are very high, and may cause the temperature of the Earth to rise dangerously because of what is known as the greenhouse effect. Satellites have also shown the destruction of the ozone layer. This layer of chemical in the upper atmosphere protects the

A Japanese newspaper which is published simultaneously in Tokyo and London. The text is transmitted directly from Japan every day by satellite.

Satellites now play an important role in air–sea rescue operations.

Earth from the deadly radiation of the sun. The erosion of the ozone layer presents one of the gravest threats to the environment in the twentieth century.

Manufacturing in space

An exciting aspect of space travel is the chance which it offers scientists to do experiments not possible on the Earth itself. It is even possible to make new or specially pure metals and chemicals in space. On Earth, gravity can make it difficult to separate or mix certain substances. In the weightless conditions of space, these same substances can be separated or mixed perfectly. Silicon crystals have been made in space, for instance. These crystals are an important part of many electronic instruments, such as computers and lasers. When silicon crystals are manufactured in an environment governed by the laws of gravity, they often have impurities which reduce their quality or make them useless. In space, perfect crystals have been produced.

Extra pure drugs can be produced in space too. During several space shuttle flights, the United States company, McDonnell Douglas, was able to produce a drug called erythropoietin. This drug helps people with diseases of the blood. Other substances have also been made on board the space shuttle. A latex

reactor produced latex particles in smaller sizes than possible on the Earth. These particles are now used as a standard measurement material by the US National Bureau of Standards. Because space flight is still so difficult, nothing can be produced in large quantities in space. Yet all of the research done in space contributes to scientific knowledge, and helps scientists and doctors to do their work in laboratories work back on Earth.

Astronauts aboard the US space shuttle conducting scientific experiments in space.

> What we have learned through space processing has given us a better understanding of the process to make it possible to be able to do a better job on the ground.
> *McDonnell Douglas*

4
The costs of space research

The United States President, John F. Kennedy, watching the spaceflight of US astronaut Alan Shepard in 1961. In spite of the high costs of space research, United States politicians did not want to lag behind the Soviet Union in the space race.

Exploring and using space is very expensive indeed. A typical US space shuttle mission costs 300 million dollars. To launch a satellite without a crew on board costs about 75 million dollars. Many people are very concerned about these high costs; they wonder how important space research really is, and suggest that all the money could be better spent, in helping the world's starving people for example. However, as we have seen, space research has also brought many benefits to humankind. The high cost of space research must be weighed against these benefits.

The space race

One of the most important reasons that so much money has been spent on space research over the last thirty years is that it gives wealthy nations and their politicians an image of success. Space research carries much political prestige. Since 1945, relations between the United States and the Soviet Union have often been hostile. Particularly during the Cold War in the 1950s, the two superpowers both built up their influence over other countries. The superpowers also began to compete with one another to have the most advanced and successful space programme.

The United States was beaten into space by the Soviet Union, which launched the first satellite in 1957. The Soviet Union was also the first nation to send a human being, Yuri Gagarin, into space. Many people admired the Soviet Union's achievements. There was great excitement about space exploration and in the 1960s the Soviet Union seemed to be leading the world. United States politicians began to feel that their country needed a more successful space programme and that the USA should achieve a space 'first' of its own. The US President John F. Kennedy started Project Apollo, the aim of which was to land a man on the Moon and return him successfully to Earth.

Project Apollo was certainly a great adventure. It demonstrated humankind's technical abilities and fulfilled its urge to explore. Twelve men walked on the Moon during six missions. They travelled 95 km over the Moon's surface on foot and in lunar vehicles and collected 2,000 samples of rock. For United States politicians, the project was a big success. All over the world, people saw television pictures of the first men on the Moon, and the United States seemed to take the lead in the space race. However, Project Apollo cost 24,000 million dollars. Even within the United States themselves, some people protested about the high cost of space exploration.

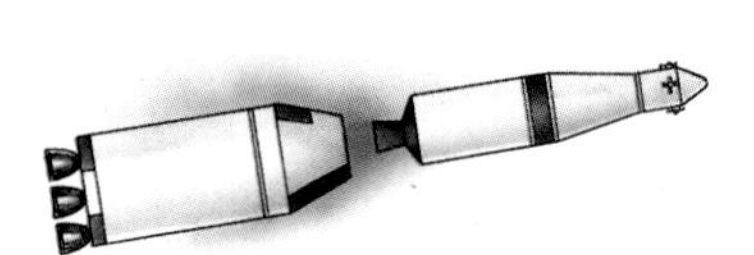

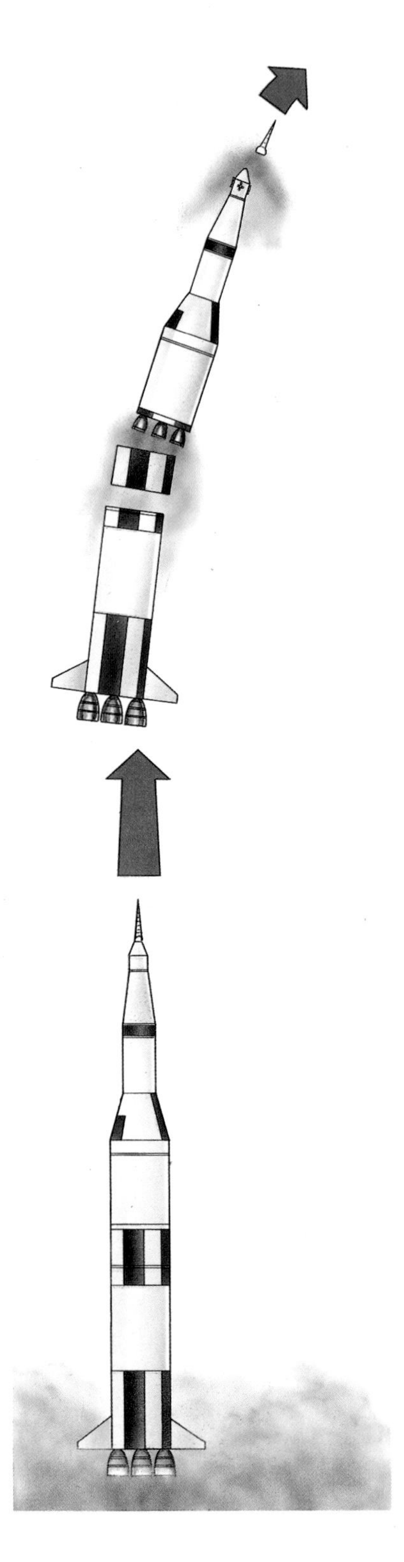

Above *The Apollo 11 spacecraft, before its historic flight.*

Left *A diagram showing how the different stages of an Apollo rocket were discarded during launch.*

One of the main reasons that the Apollo missions were so expensive was that the Apollo spacecraft could only be used once. Most of the spacecraft was discarded during the course of a mission. When an Apollo mission was launched, it began with a 111 metre high Saturn booster with the small Apollo spacecraft on top of it. By the end of the mission all that remained of the whole rocket-spacecraft combination was a 3.5 m high command module containing the three-man crew. Even that command module was placed straight into a museum, never to be used again. An Apollo space mission was rather like throwing away an airliner after one passenger-carrying flight! Not surprisingly, there were demands that a new type of spacecraft, which could be used over and over again, should be developed.

The space shuttle – a reusable spaceship?

Over the past two decades, the demand for a reusable spacecraft has led to the development of the United States space shuttle, which made its maiden voyage in 1981. However, the space shuttle is by no means completely reusable, and its development has demonstrated exactly how difficult it will be to produce a vehicle that can fly into space just like an airliner. The shuttle can only be launched with the help of rockets. Each shuttle has a huge fuel tank which is disposed of during the launch. Moreover, the shuttle is still neither a routine nor a completely safe spacecraft; in 1986, the *Challenger* space shuttle exploded during take-off, killing its seven crew members.

In fact, the space shuttle is a very fragile, technical test plane. It took nine years and 15,000 million dollars to produce, yet will still not be fully operational for many years to come. Everyone agrees that, in the long term, a reusable spacecraft is necessary, but who would be ready to invest the time and huge sums of money needed to build it? Governments and industrialists are more willing to put money into developing telecommunications or other satellites, which quickly make profits. For the time being, humankind continues to exploit space much as it always has done – by throwing away satellite and spacecraft launch vehicles.

Justifying the cost of space research

The cost of some space research can be easily justified. Communications satellites make big profits for their owners and the satellite operators are willing to spend between 50 and 120 million dollars just to have a satellite placed in orbit. However, other satellites do not make so much money and their worth is not so easy to measure. Many kinds of satellite do not make much commercial profit at all. The profit from an astronomical satellite, which discovers a new type of star, is the knowledge it provides. Weather satellites are of great value, because they make possible very accurate weather forecasts. By forecasting typhoons or hurricanes, they may save thousands of lives and millions of dollars. Yet they do not make money directly, and governments rather than private companies must provide the large sums of money which these satellites cost to operate.

In recent years, space projects have been increasingly justified in terms of the money they can earn for individual governments. Millions of dollars have been spent to finance the space shuttle, for instance, because the United States government believed that the shuttle could eventually be used as a satellite launch vehicle. However, despite the successes achieved by the space-shuttle programme, it is not simple to make quick and easy profits from space.

One of the best-known developments in recent space technology is the introduction of Direct Broadcasting Television Satellites. Some people claim that these satellites are causing a revolution in television viewing. Viewers can place aerials on the roofs of their homes which receive television programmes direct from satellites. In the United States, satellite channels are already in operation and are fairly successful, although not as popular as cable television. From late 1989, independent satellite-television channels will be available to British viewers too. Some of these channels will be funded by advertising, but to receive others, viewers will have to pay a special fee. The operators hope to make large profits, and one of the new satellite TV companies, British Satellite Broadcasting, is investing over £600 million in two satellites. The company hopes to have two million

Atlantis
NASA
United States

Above *An artist's impression of a possible future European space shuttle, which could take off into low Earth orbits from European airports.*

Left *The United States space shuttle* Atlantis *just about to touch down on the runway after a test flight.*

viewers watching its programmes by 1990. But are its predictions realistic? Will British viewers be willing to pay for another twelve channels, when they can already watch four channels for the price of a single licence fee? In Europe, satellite television already seems to be unsuccessful, and satellite stations in France and West Germany are finding it difficult to attract viewers. Even British Satellite Broadcasting admits that it does not expect to make a profit until 1995.

Companies that want to make a profit using remote-sensing satellites face similar problems to broadcasting companies. They must pay huge sums of money to launch satellites, without being sure that anyone will want to buy the information that they provide. Up until now, remote sensors have always been subsidized by governments, but as they become more powerful, they may become more profitable; and a recent British report listed six ways in which remote sensors could make money, including mapping and monitoring pollution.

Another possible way of making money in space is by the development of space factories. Recent space-shuttle flights have already shown how certain new substances can be manufactured in space. In the future, it may be possible to use orbiting space factories to manufacture these products which cannot be made perfectly on Earth. The United States plans to build an international space station called *Freedom* in 1996, which will research the possibility of manufacturing in space. But will there really soon be space factories churning out drugs and electrical components on a large scale? Space factories would be very expensive to build and would take many years to develop. *Freedom* itself will cost 30,000 million dollars and is only the first step towards the regular construction of space factories. The real benefit of this kind of research will probably be the way it adds to scientific knowledge in general.

In space manufacturing, as in many other areas of space research, governments face a

A photograph of hurricane cloud formations taken from a weather satellite.

In the studios of Sky Channel, a direct satellite broadcasting station whose programmes can be received in many European countries.

dilemma. They may want to invest money to develop the opportunities that spaceflight offers. But if the benefits of their research are uncertain, or will not be felt until well into the next century, they may also be accused of wasting their country's money.

While no one expects giant space foundries to turn out quantities of manufactured product in the near future, scientists do expect this research to uncover compounds whose properties are of great benefit.

National Aeronautics and Space Administration (NASA)

Protest against the expense of space research is often greatest when people are aware of other world problems which demand a lot of money. Space research can seem wasteful when television news bulletins show pictures of famine such as that experienced in Ethiopia in 1984. However, it is one of the ironies

A satellite dish on the roof of a restaurant in the United States.

of modern life that these pictures are brought so strikingly to the rest of the world by the space technology which in itself seems so wasteful. In fact, satellites can even be used to help to solve the problem of starvation in underdeveloped countries. Bob Geldof's famous *Live Aid* concert raised about 50 million dollars to help the victims of the Ethiopian famine. The concert was so successful only because it was broadcast throughout the world by satellite. Moreover, the food and supplies provided by *Live Aid* were delivered by trucks driving along remote roads which had been mapped by satellites.

An artist's impression of what the projected US space station Freedom *may look like when in orbit above the Earth.*

LIVE
AID

Above *A Kenyan doctor treating an undernourished child at a famine relief centre in Ethiopia. Although space research may seem wasteful in comparison with famine relief, satellites can be used to tackle problems in the developing world.*

Left *The Live Aid concert held in London in 1985.*

> I say there is something wrong with our sense of priorities when scientists have to defend with almost every breath the millions being spent on space research in a nation that spends five times as much for tobacco and cosmetics.
> *Dr. James Fletcher, NASA Administrator*

The amount of money 'wasted' on space research must also be compared with the amounts spent in other ways in the world's wealthiest nations. Millions of dollars are spent on weapons. Millions more are smoked away, drunk or spent on cosmetics; in the United States, more than six times more money is spent on tobacco, alcohol and cosmetics than on space research.

Space research attracts a lot of public attention, because events such as the space shuttle missions make spectacular news. Yet money is spent in other, much less constructive ways, and receives little attention in newspapers or on television. The cost of space research is put into perspective by the fact that US citizens spend more on their pets annually than their government does on space programmes.

5
The growing problem of space debris

A satellite launch using the European Ariane *rocket. Every time a satellite is launched, thousands of tiny pieces of space debris are also sent into orbit.*

What causes space debris?

Because satellites are so expensive, anyone who operates a satellite in space wants it to remain in orbit for as long as possible. Whenever feasible, satellites are sent into an orbit that is high enough to make sure that atmospheric drag will not bring the satellite down to earth too soon, before it stops operating. However, putting a satellite into high orbit causes a problem. When the satellite stops working it stays in orbit for hundreds of years, rather than falling back to Earth and burning up in the Earth's atmosphere. The number of 'dead' satellites still in orbit is growing and only five per cent of all orbiting satellites are actually operational. The Earth's orbit is becoming a junk-yard filled with space debris.

Dead satellites are not the only debris in space. During every satellite launch, all kinds of waste are delivered into orbit along with the satellite itself. The rocket stage which propels the satellite often goes into orbit. So do the nuts, bolts or screws that are sometimes released when the satellite separates from its stage, and its protective nose cap. More debris is created as the satellite is exposed to the intense heat, cold and radiation of space. It sheds bits of paint and its protective layering or insulation. Rocket fuel can be yet another source of space debris. As the fuel burns, aluminium-oxide dust forms in the rocket exhaust and later collects in space along with all the other bits and pieces of debris.

Sometimes, the unused fuel in the tanks of orbiting rocket stages can explode, creating more debris. Since 1973, the upper stages of seven disused orbiting Delta rockets have exploded, creating 1,230 pieces of debris. On other occasions, satellites themselves have been known to explode. The Soviet satellite Cosmos 1423, for example, exploded in space during December 1982, probably because there was a fault in its own engine.

To make matters worse, satellites have even been deliberately exploded in orbit. In 1987, an orbiting Soviet photographic spy satellite became faulty. Its recoverable film capsule could not be commanded to make a controlled return to a specially planned landing zone in the Soviet Union. Soviet scientists knew that the satellite would re-enter the Earth's atmosphere eventually, and that when it did, the capsule might land outside Soviet territory and be recovered by a foreign intelligence agency. It was decided therefore to trigger the satellite's self-destruct mechanism. Even more space debris was created .

Yet another source of debris has been anti-satellite weapons, which have been tested in space by both the United States and the Soviet Union. One kind of anti-satellite weapon destroys its target by firing a shower of metal pellets; both the destroyed target and the metal pellets become dangerous space debris.

In addition to the nearly 2,000 satellites still in orbit, most of which are dead, there are a further 5,500 large-sized pieces of orbiting space debris that can be tracked by special stations on Earth. There is also a huge amount of debris that cannot be tracked because it is too small. Scientists have estimated that there are over 30,000 pieces of small debris, between the size of a marble and a football. There are also trillions of tiny paint flakes, and millions of trillions of particles of dust. Altogether, explosions in space have accounted for about half of this space debris.

Most debris is found somewhere between 300 km and 1,000 km above the Earth, the space into which most satellites are launched. Because satellites are launched to different heights and cross the Equator at different angles, the debris speeds around the Earth in different directions and in a wide variety of different orbits. Satellites and debris are constantly crisscrossing each other in the space above the Earth. Moreover, if a rocket stage explodes, its debris is scattered in all directions, adding to the confusing crisscross.

Because space debris travels at such high speeds, it represents a potential threat to anyone in space. It is quite possible that sometime in the future, a space-walking astronaut could be hit and killed by a piece of space debris. Even a tiny flake of paint, travelling at 10 km per second, could puncture an astronaut's spacesuit and cause him an agonising death. Scientists maintain that the chances of such an accident happening are about 20,000 to one, but the odds are shortening every day as the amount of space debris increases. United States astronauts have already had one lucky escape. In 1983, the space shuttle *Challenger* was struck by a piece of paint. The paint was only 0.2 mm in diameter and hit Challenger at a speed of 5 km per second. However, it still made a mark on the cockpit window. A larger piece of debris, travelling even faster, could have smashed the window completely. The air inside the shuttle would have been sucked out into the vacuum of space, and the whole crew would have been killed.

An artist's impression which shows an ASAT (Anti-satellite) weapon showering a target with tiny pellets.

Despite the dangers of space debris, no one has done anything yet to try to solve the problem, and it becomes more serious every day. Experts say that by the year 2038, there will be 96,000 trackable pieces of space debris in orbit. This figure does not take account of the many millions of small objects undetected by tracking systems. There is a fear that there will be a cascade effect in the increase of debris.

Pieces of debris will collide with each other, splitting into many more pieces and multiplying the amount of debris in space. Collisions are particularly bad, because they create even more debris than an explosion. A 3,000 kg satellite hit by a large piece of debris at very high speed would break into ten times more fragments than if it simply exploded. There is a real danger that the lower Earth orbits could become so cluttered up with debris that they will become totally unusable.

> The insidious character of the debris hazard is the possibility of a cascade effect, rendering low Earth orbit unusable.
>
> *W. Mendall and D. Kessler in a NASA report, Limits to Growth in Low Earth Orbit*

The General Electric SP-100 Space Nuclear Reactor System. This nuclear reactor could be used to supply power to future satellites, increasing the amount of radioactive material in space.

Nuclear waste in space

The problem of space debris is made more dangerous and worrying by the fact that some of the debris is radioactive. Most satellites are solar powered. Solar cells on the outside of the satellite convert sunlight into electricity. However, nuclear power is used on satellites that need large amounts of electricity. For example, Rorsat, the Soviet radar ocean spy satellite, is nuclear powered. It contains a nuclear reactor that creates electricity from the heat coming from radioactive uranium in its nuclear power-plant. There are now over fifty radioactive satellites in orbit, and several have fallen back to Earth, contaminating the Earth's surface and its atmosphere.

Normally, when a Rorsat satellite has completed its mission, the power-plant, containing the radioactive core, is fired into a higher storage orbit where it will remain for hundreds of years. The core itself is ejected even further away from the Earth and its radioactivity dies down as it remains in space. Meanwhile, the main spacecraft fires its retrorockets, and burns up as it re-enters the atmosphere.

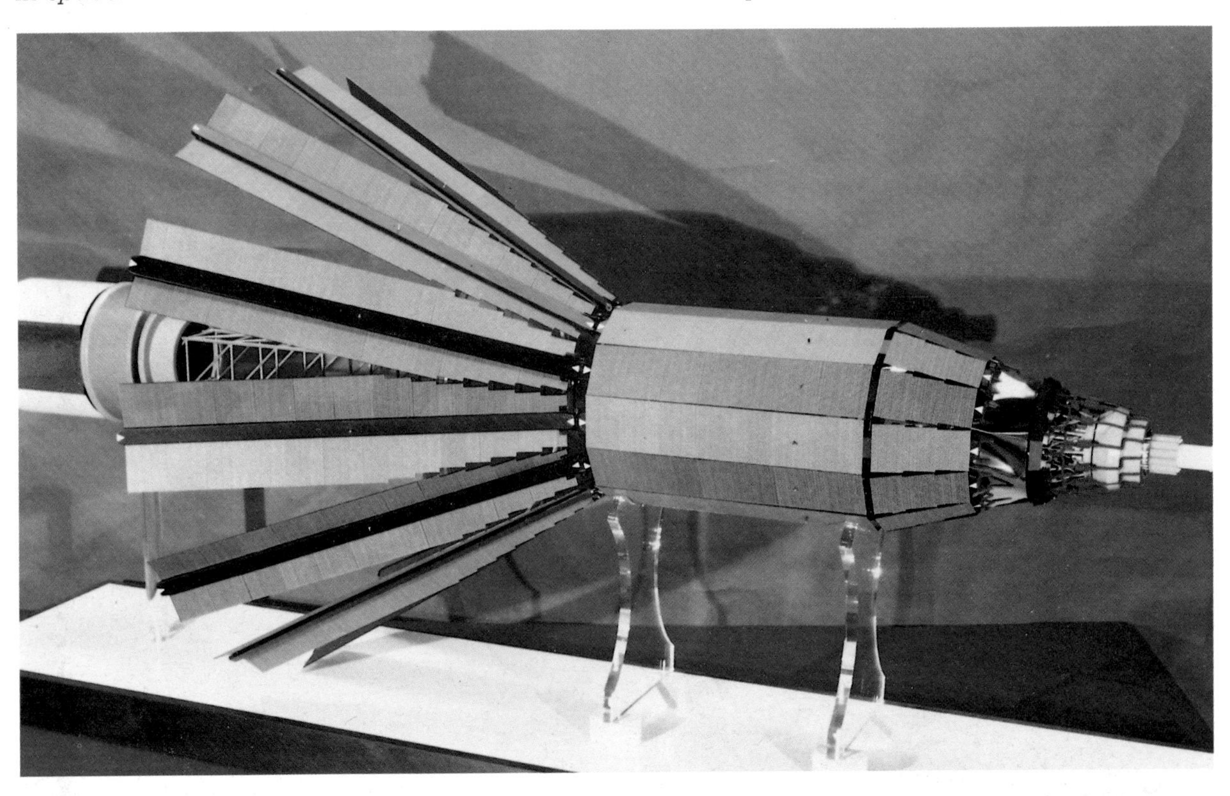

Unfortunately, the operation does not always go according to plan. In 1978, the Rorsat, Cosmos 954, could not eject its powerplant into a higher orbit. The whole satellite re-entered the Earth's atmosphere and the radioactive core was protected by the outer casing of its powerplant and survived the re-entry. Radioactive debris was scattered over remote parts of Canada; it was only by chance that it did not land in a more highly populated area.

The Cosmos 954 crash made people more aware of the dangers of nuclear powered satellites. The worldwide concern caused the Soviet Union to design a safety feature on the Rorsat. Now, even if the main operation fails, a back-up system fires the radioactive core into a higher orbit before re-entry, so that it is impossible for the satellite to shower radioactive material over the Earth.

> The dangers of space debris and the nuclear contamination of space are being treated with a yawn by the space community.
>
> *Parker Temple, The Pentagon*

There is even space debris on the Moon left behind after the Apollo landings.

Solutions for the space debris problem

Although it is possible to design extra safety devices for nuclear satellites, there is still no easy solution to the problem of space debris as a whole. All future satellites could be equipped with systems that make sure that when they stop working, they are sent back into the atmosphere and burn up. However, it may be difficult to activate this re-entry system once the rest of the satellite has ceased to operate.

Another solution would be to give each satellite a limited working lifetime under international law. At a planned time it would have to be sent back into the atmosphere. Unfortunately, satellite operators would object strongly to such a law, since they would lose money by being forced to destroy a working satellite.

Some scientists have suggested that larger dead satellites could be collected by space shuttles and brought back to Earth. Others have suggested the building of a giant 'fly catcher' satellite, with a large surface area, rather like a sail, to which debris would stick. The satellite and all the attached debris could then be deliberately destroyed during re-entry. Yet another possible solution would be to completely destroy small pieces of space debris using laser beams fired from the Earth. However, all these solutions would be very expensive, and are still way beyond the technology which scientists already possess.

There have been severe warnings about the problem of space debris in reports by the US Pentagon, NASA and other organizations. But neither the United States nor the Soviet Union has announced any major plans to limit the amount of space debris. There are fears that trying to control space debris could slow down new and exciting projects and reduce the profitability of satellites. For the time being, humankind continues to fill the Earth's orbit with rubbish. There is even space debris from the Apollo missions on the surface of the Moon.

The problem of debris in space is treated in much the same way as the problem of pollution on Earth. People try to reduce the amount they pollute the environment. Yet many problems are left for future generations to solve. Space debris may today be nothing more than a small inconvenience for space users. But if nothing is done soon, the pollution of the Earth's orbit could spell the end of scientific developments and the exploitation of space. In future centuries, humankind may have the technology to build spacecraft which can travel across the universe. But the launching of these spacecraft would be impossible because of the massive cloud of space debris which had been left behind by past generations.

From the outset, the Strategic Defence Initiative received strong support from the then United States President, Ronald Reagan.

6 The militarization of space

In recent years, the most controversial space projects have been those which plan to develop weapons in space. In 1983, the then President, Ronald Reagan, announced that the United States would begin research into a space weapons system. Using weapons in space, the United States would develop a system to destroy any attacking enemy missiles. The system is officially called the Strategic Defence Initiative, or SDI, but it is more often called the Star Wars Project. If it meets the target set by President Reagan, it will become operational in 1999.

A photograph of Moscow, the Soviet capital, taken from space by a spy satellite.

> Mastery of space is an important prerequisite for achieving victory in war.
> *Dictionary of Basic Military Terms, USSR, 1965*

Weapons in space

Although space weapons are a controversial issue today, in fact there has been military activity in space for over thirty years. In 1959, just two years into the Space Age, the first of many military satellites, called Discoverer, went into orbit. Discoverer satellites carried a recoverable capsule containing a camera which took the first spy pictures from space. Today, over 80 per cent of all satellites launched have some kind of military use.

There have also been operational weapons in space since before the Strategic Defence Initiative was even begun. The United States developed and tested an anti-satellite weapon in the early 1980s. It was launched from a high flying jet and wastefully destroyed a functioning US military target satellite. The Soviet Union has developed similar anti-satellite weapons. Space mines have been launched and flown close to Soviet target satellites. The target has then been destroyed by a spray of debris as the weapon satellite was deliberately exploded. The United States has even claimed that one of its satellites has been put out of action by a laser beam which was fired from a secret Soviet military base.

The commonest types of military satellite in use today are spy satellites. They take photographs from space on film which is returned to Earth in a recoverable capsule. As the film must be retrieved and developed quickly, every effort is made to get the capsule to make pinpoint landings. The United States even goes as far as to catch the capsule in mid-air before it lands. Photographs taken from spy satellites have very high resolution, and even small objects can be seen from space. Photographs taken by the US Big Bird satellite can show objects as small as one metre in diameter. However, the claim sometimes made for the Big Bird satellites, that they can read the headline of a newspaper being read in Moscow's Red Square, is not quite true.

Most of the spy satellites that have been launched belong to the Soviet Union. Out of a total number of about 120 satellite launches worldwide every year, around 60 will be Soviet military satellites. The United States paints a threatening picture of Soviet intentions in space by quoting this high number of Soviet launches. In fact, the United States probably carries out just as much espionage from satellites as the Soviet Union, but in a different way. The United States launches a fairly small number of satellites, each of which is equipped to carry out a variety of duties in orbit. In contrast, the Soviet Union launches a whole range of low, medium and high resolution spy satellites, each of which does one specific task. Although this system is expensive, it is very flexible, since the Soviet Union can custom launch satellites on special operations when necessary.

Right *An antenna dish, used by the US military to receive signals sent out by navigational satellites.*

Below *A mobile system for picking up signals from a navigational satellite.*

WARNING
RESTRICTED AREA
AUTHORIZED
PERSONNEL
ONLY

A diagram which shows how future laser weapons might be used to destroy an attacking enemy missile.

Spy satellites have become vitally important to the peacetime military operations of many countries. Their great advantage is that they enable the United States and Soviet Union to know what each other is doing. Any new missile sites, for example, can be seen from space. However, spy satellites have also been used during armed combat. Egypt was supplied with Soviet satellite images during its many conflicts with Israel during the 1960s and 1970s. The Soviet satellites which supplied these images were launched specifically to overfly the battle zone when lighting conditions were perfect for photography.

In addition to spying and reconnaissance, satellites have many other military uses. Communications satellites can prove vital to a nation's armed forces. They enable a troop commander to talk directly to his headquarters from anywhere else in the world. During the Falklands conflict between Britain and Argentina in 1982, Mrs Thatcher, the British Prime Minister, was kept in direct touch with British troops on the Falkland Islands by using a military communications satellite.

Navigation satellites have military uses too. One navigation system allows a troop commander to work out his exact position using a small portable computer which fits into a rucksack. The computer collects signals from three orbiting navigation satellites and uses them to work out its own position on the Earth's surface.

Military weather satellites provide precise weather reports for armed services. In a similar way, ocean survey satellites watch ice and icebergs, so that naval vessels can pass quickly around the North and South Poles. Early warning satellites are also very important. They provide information to military headquarters about missile launches all over the world. This information can be analysed and a missile can be identified to make sure that it is not part of an enemy attack.

Another use of military satellites is to receive and store intelligence messages from secret agents. Messages are transmitted to a satellite as it passes above a secret agent. The message is stored and then played back to Earth when the satellite passes over military headquarters.

Some satellites, called electronic intelligence satellites, or elints for short, pick up all kinds of radio signals as they pass over hostile territory. They can sift out 'rubbish' such as radio noise, and identify any important pieces of intelligence information.

The Strategic Defence Initiative

Although there are so many different kinds of military activity in space, most people were not especially aware of military satellites until President Reagan announced the Strategic Defence Initiative (SDI) in 1983. However, since the beginning of SDI, everyone has become more concerned about the weapons that could turn space into a battleground.

The aim of SDI is to prove that the United States has the technology to develop what US officials call a 'layered defence system'. This system would be able to destroy any enemy missile during every stage of its attack; from its launch and ascent to the time close to the end of its flight.

According to the Strategic Defence Initiative Organization in Washington, there are several areas of SDI research. Surveillance satellites form an important part of the defence system. They would be used to spot an enemy missile by continually spying on hostile launch pads. The satellites would track the missile in flight

A diagram showing how kinetic energy weapons could be launched in space to intercept an attacking missile.

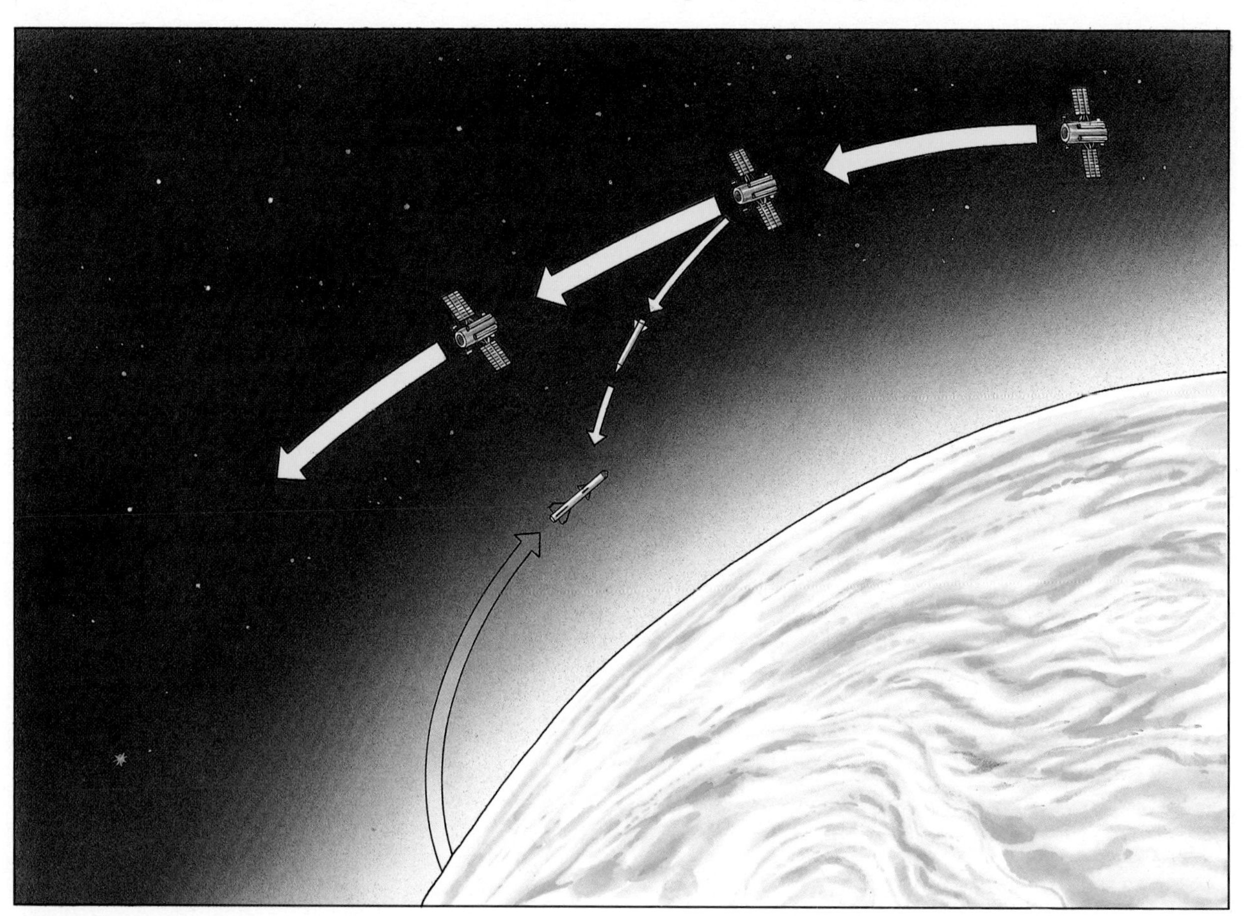

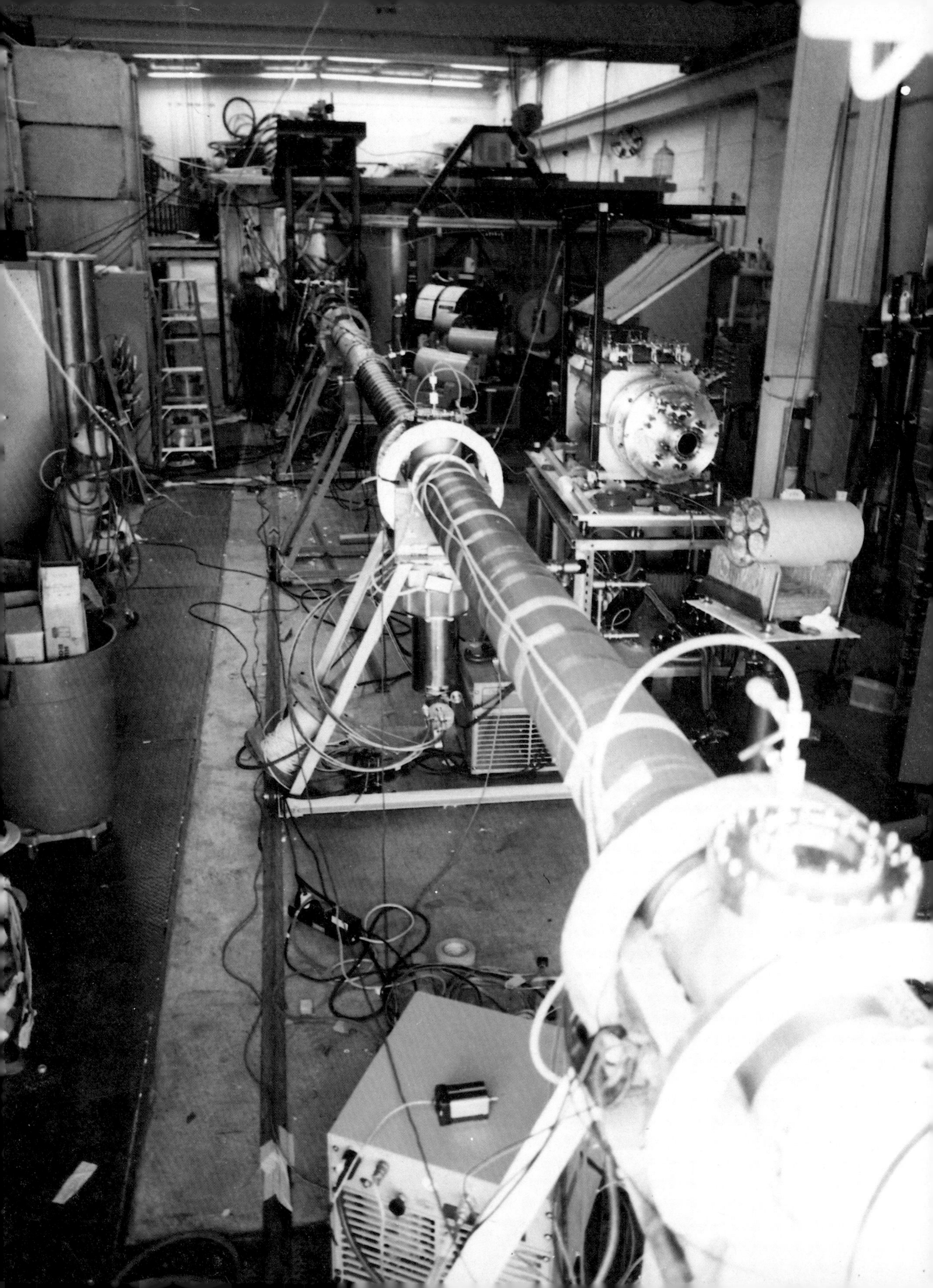

Above *The electromagnetic launcher developed by SDI researchers. The launcher can fire small bullets into space at very high speeds, using electric and magnetic energy as opposed to rockets which use chemical energy.*

Left *A prototype of an electron beam weapon, devised by US scientists.*

and work out the best way to destroy it. Another satellite would examine the missile as it continued its flight. An on-board computer could tell whether the missile carried a warhead or whether it were just a harmless decoy. This satellite would also predict the missile's target.

The Strategic Defence Initiative Organization is researching two kinds of weapon that could actually destroy enemy missiles. One section of research concentrates on laser beams, very strong beams of light that can travel a great distance. SDI hopes to develop a gun that fires a laser beam which could vaporize missiles. Kinetic energy weapons would also be used. They are more like conventional weapons and could be fired from the ground or from space, and would physically destroy attacking missiles. These kinetic energy weapons are the part of the SDI programme which is closest to completion.

In contrast to the United States, the Soviet Union says that it is not researching one single large-scale space defence programme. However, the United States claims that the Soviet ion does have a large space weapons project, and believes that some Soviet research is more advanced than its own.

A test carried out by SDI scientists which proved that it would be possible to destroy objects using a laser beam.

According to the US Department of Defence report, *Soviet Space Power*, the Soviet Union operates a large laser beam research programme. This programme is believed to involve 10,000 scientists and engineers, and takes place at the Sary Shagan Missile Test Centre. In addition to a laser beam system that can stop satellites from working, the United States believes that the Soviet Union will also be able to operate a space laser weapon successfully before the end of the century.

Soviet scientists have also studied particle beam weapons. These weapons are similar to lasers, but use extremely small particles rather than concentrated light. Particles are shot out into space in a beam. The United States claims that within the next decade, Soviet particle beam weapons will be capable of destroying the vital electronic components of orbiting satellites. The United States is itself now beginning to research particle beams, though much of its own work is based upon that which was carried out by the Soviet Union during the 1960s and 1970s.

The Soviet Union may have tested other types of space weapon too. Soviet scientists have investigated the use of very high frequency radio waves which can damage the electronic parts of a satellite. They have tested an optical system that can be used to spot enemy spacecraft. In the 1960s, they also developed a kinetic energy gun that shot small, heavy metal pellets towards its target. The gun could fire streams of pellets, like a blunderbuss, up to 60 km through space at a speed of almost 25 km per second.

No one doubts that both the United States and the Soviet Union are researching space weapons. Yet it is very difficult for any observer to know all the real details about this research. Newspapers and television reports often discuss SDI and Soviet research, but information about top secret weapons is limited. The issue is made more confusing to the onlooker, because both superpowers accuse each other of doing more advanced and dangerous research. The Soviet Union says that it does not have a large programme like the Strategic Defence Initiative. The United States replies by pointing towards Soviet research into other kinds of space weapons. In fact it is probably true to say that both sides feel threatened. Each superpower is afraid that the other may have more advanced technology. They both fear that the other will make important discoveries first.

Both superpowers also claim that their research is for defensive purposes only. SDI, for instance, is always presented as a way of defending the United States from enemy attack. However, virtually all of the new space weapons, in both the United States and the Soviet Union, could be used to attack enemies as well as for defence. Politicians representing each of the two superpowers often make illogical claims for their country's space research. They insist that their own space research is for defensive purposes only; yet they say that similar research in the other country is threatening and offensive.

> We must not cede space control to the Soviet Union or to any other power that could use it to coerce national security or restrict our liberties.
>
> *Caspar Weinberger, US Secretary for Defence, 1987*

Part of an experiment by SDI scientists researching particle beam weapons.

In the West, the Strategic Defence Initiative has already been the subject of much discussion in newspapers and on television. Some scientists have claimed that SDI is a waste of money, and that space weapons will never work. Other people have argued that the project is dangerous. Although SDI weapons are supposed to be used only for defence, they could lead to a new arms race in space between the United States and the Soviet Union. Some people believe that the very existence of new weapons is a threat to peace and makes the world a more dangerous place in which to live. There are also fears that if a Strategic Defence System is ever built, it could easily go wrong. It could one day confuse a civilian airliner with an enemy missile and shoot it down by mistake.

Other people believe that there are strong arguments in favour of developing space weapons. If both superpowers have similar weapons, there will be a balance of power between them. Politicians also argue that any nation has the right to develop the best defences that it can. Spy satellites, in particular, do seem to make the world a more secure place. They certainly make it very difficult for any country to build major new military bases in secret.

US officials insist that the SDI programme is for research only, and that the US government will have to make a separate decision to actually build SDI weapons. Nonetheless, humankind will soon have the ability to conduct warfare in space. Many people believe that this development is the most harmful way in which space is exploited.

Many people are opposed to research into space weapons. Here Bruce Kent and E.P. Thompson, active in the Campaign for Nuclear Disarmament, protest outside the British Parliament with Darth Vader, a character from the film Star Wars.

7 Space – the final frontier?

This book has tried to describe some of the effects of humankind's voyages into space over the past thirty years. There can be few people in the world whose lives have not been changed somehow as a result of the exploitation of space.

Perhaps the greatest change of all has been the growth in humankind's knowledge and understanding of the universe in which we live. If, for example, you read a book about the solar system written in the 1950s and then compare it with one written today, you will get a dramatic and vivid impression of how space technology has improved our understanding of other planets. We now know that Mercury, the closest planet to the Sun, has craters like the Moon; Venus is covered in thick white clouds and has a scorching hot surface. Space probes have photographed the moons of Jupiter and examined the rings of Saturn. The *Voyager II* probe has travelled even further afield, to Uranus and Neptune.

The Voyager 11 *space probe , which is exploring the outer reaches of our solar system before going on into deep space.*

The Hubble Space Telescope, which will enable scientists to see further into space.

In 1986, the European spacecraft Giotto flew right inside Halley's Comet. It found out what kind of gases the comet contained. This information has helped scientists to understand how our solar system was formed. The new Hubble Space Telescope will also help scientists to learn more about the space which lies beyond our own solar system. It can peer fifteen times further into space than is possible with telescopes on Earth.

By learning more about the Universe, people have begun to think about their own planet, the Earth, in different ways. From the Earth itself, the world can seem a very divided place. Some people have great wealth, others are desperately poor. Every day, somewhere in the world, people are fighting each other.

Yet photographs taken from spaceships have shown our planet as one beautiful blue and white globe. Astronauts who have seen the Earth from a distance have realized how small and fragile it is, set in the vast and hostile emptiness of space. They realized the importance of people learning to live together in harmony, all taking care of the limited resources of their tiny planet.

Some of the problems that have been encountered in space will be difficult to overcome. Space debris will be hard to clear away; the superpowers may increase their stock of space weapons; and it may still take many years to develop a totally reusable spacecraft. Yet even these problems have a beneficial side, because they test humankind's ingenuity and stretch it to its limits.

> The Earth looks like a small oasis in the blackness of space.
>
> *James Lovell, astronaut on the Apollo 8 mission, 1968*

Throughout the ages, humans have struggled to learn more about the world in which they live, and to master their environment. The human race seems to have an inborn need to meet new challenges and explore the unknown. In the words of the famous television programme, *Star Trek*, humans have a need 'to go where no man has gone before'. Space travel is one way in which the human race can fulfil its need to expand and develop.

The first spacecraft were launched barely thirty years ago. Since 1957, space research has made enormous progress. Scientists are constantly making discoveries and seeing new opportunities in space. No one knows what the next thirty years may bring. However, the problems of space debris and increasing numbers of weapons in space could seriously disturb tomorrow's space research. Space scientists and governments are faced by a great challenge. They must make sure that they do not exploit space in a harmful and thoughtless way. Unless they use space carefully today, humankind may not be able to achieve its full potential in space in the future.

The Earth, the 'small oasis' in space on which we live. Space research has made us more aware of how fragile our environment is.

Glossary

Anti-satellite weapon A weapon which destroys satellites.

Astronomical satellite A satellite fitted with a telescope and other equipment which studies space.

Atmosphere The layer of gases which surround the Earth.

Atmospheric drag The way in which the atmosphere slows down a satellite which is in a low orbit.

Cable television Television channels supplied through a cable and for which people must pay a special fee.

Cold War The period during the 1950s and 1960s when relations between the governments of the United States and Soviet Union were very poor.

Comet A lump of dust and frozen gasses that moves around the Sun.

Elint An intelligence satellite which picks up radio signals.

Geostationary orbit A satellite in geostationary orbit rotates at the same speed as the Earth, and remains fixed above one place on the Earth's surface.

Greenhouse effect The way in which an increase in carbon dioxide levels is causing the temperature of the Earth to rise dangerously high.

Kinetic energy weapon A weapon which destroys its target using a physical object, such as a bullet.

Laser beam A beam of very intense, powerful light.

Latex reactor A machine which makes a type of artificial rubber.

Low polar orbit An orbit close to the surface of the Earth, in which a satellite passes directly over the North and South Pole.

Meteor A stony object that travels through space.

Meteorite A stony object that lands on Earth from space. Meteorites also fall on other planets and their moons.

Ozone layer The layer of gas which protects the Earth from radiation from the Sun.

Orbit The path that a satellite follows as it moves around a planet or star.

Remote sensing Surveying the surface of the Earth from space.

Retrorocket A small rocket which sends a spacecraft backwards, or alters its direction.

Satellite A spacecraft which moves around, or orbits, a planet or star.

Solar system A star and the planets which move around it.

Space probe A spacecraft sent out to explore other planets or parts of space.

Strategic Defence Initiative The United States research programme to develop a system of defences using satellites and weapons in space.

Superpower A very powerful country. Usually refers either to the United States or the Soviet Union.

Telecommunications Long-distance communications.

Vacuum A space which is completely empty.

Vaporize To turn something to vapour or destroy it completely.

Picture acknowledgements

Barnaby's Picture Library 10, 18; British Telecom 14; Camera Press 32; Melanie Friend 42; Tim Furniss *cover, frontispiece,* 7, 16, 20, 21, 24, 28; Photri 15, 24, 34, 35, 43, 44; The Research House 29, 40; Strategic Defence Initiative Organization 30, 38, 39, 41; Topham Picture Library 26, 27; Wayland Picture Library 8, 13, 17, 23, 31; ZEFA 6, 12, 22, 33, 45. All artwork is by Peter Bull.

Further information

If you wish to find out more about some of the subjects covered in this book, you might find the following addresses useful:

National Space Society,
922, Pennsylvanian Avenue SE,
Washington DC. 20003,
USA.

British Interplanetary Society,
27–29 South Lambeth Road,
London SW8 1SZ,
United Kingdom.

National Aeronautics and Space Administration (NASA),
Maryland Avenue,
Washington DC. 20546,
USA.

Australian Space Office,
PO Box 269,
Civic Square,
Canberra.
A.C.T. 2608,
Australia.

Astronaut Program Office,
National Research Office,
Building M60, Room B21,
Montreal Road,
Ottawa,
Ontario. K1A OR6.
Canada.

Campaign for Nuclear Disarmament,
22–24, Underwood Street,
London. N1 7JG.
United Kingdom.

Books to read

Baker, David *The Shape of Wars to Come* (Hamlyn, 1982)

Furniss, Tim *Our Future in Space* (Wayland, 1985)

Furniss, Tim *Space Exploitation* (Batsford, 1984)

Furniss, Tim *Space Today* (Kaye and Ward, 1978)

Gatland, Kenneth *Space Technology* (Salamander, 1981)

Lambert, David *The Earth in Space* (Wayland, 1988)

Lewis, Richard *Space Exploration* (Salamander, 1983)

Moore, Patrick *Man's Future in Space* (Wayland, 1981)

Index

Anti-satellite weapons 29, 33
Apollo space project 10, 12, 17–18, 19, 32
Ariane 28
Atmosphere 8–10
Atmospheric drag 10, 28

British Satellite Broadcasting 19

Campaign for Nuclear Disarmament 42
Cold War 17
Cosmos 1423 28
Cosmos 954 crash 31

Drugs 15, 22

Egypt, war with Israel, 36
Ethiopia, famine in 24–5

Falklands Conflict 36
France 21

Gagarin, Yuri 17
Geldof, Bob 25
Giotto spacecraft 44
Gravity 10, 15
Greenhouse effect 14

Halley's Comet 44
Heatshields 10
Hubble space telescope 44

Israel, war with Egypt 36

Kennedy, President John F. 17
Kinetic energy weapons 37, 39, 41

Lasers 15, 33, 36, 39, 40
Live Aid 25

Manufacturing in space 14–16, 22
Mapping 6, 14, 25
Meteorites 8
Moon 6, 10, 12, 17, 32

Orbits 10–11, 28
  circular 10
  eccentric 10
  geostationary 12, 13, 14
  low polar 10, 14
Ozone layer 8, 14

Particle beam weapons 41
Pollution 6, 14, 32

Radiation 8, 15, 28
Radioactivity 30–31
Reagan, President Ronald 33, 37
Rockets 7, 10, 13, 19, 28
Rorsat 30–31

Sary Shagan Missile Test Centre 40
Satellites 6, 7, 10, 24, 28, 29
  astronomical 19
  Big Bird 34
  communications 6, 12, 13, 19
  direct broadcasting 13, 19, 23
  Discoverer 33
  early warning 36
  electronic intelligence (ELINTs) 37
  Intelsat 8, 13
  military communications 36
  navigation 12, 34–36
  nuclear powered 30–32
  ocean survey 36
  remote sensing 6, 14, 21
  search and rescue 14–15
  secret launches 12
  solar powered 30
  spy 12, 29, 30, 33–7, 42
  Syncom 13
  Telstar 13
  weather forecasting 6, 14, 19, 22
Silicon crystals 15
Solar system 6, 43
Soyuz spacecraft 10
Space debris 6, 28–32, 44
Space probes 6, 43
Space shuttle 7, 10, 15–17, 19–21, 32
  Challenger 19, 29
Space stations 6,
  Freedom 25
Sputnik I 6
Star Wars see Strategic Defence Initiative
Strategic Defence Initiative 33, 37–9, 41–2

Television pictures, transmission of 13
Thatcher, Prime Minister Margaret 36

USA
  Amount of money spent on space research 27
  causing space debris 29, 32
  Moon landing 12
  relations with USSR 17
  weapons research 6, 33–42

USSR
  causing space debris 28–9, 32
  relations with USA 17
  space exploration 6
  weapons research 6, 33–42

Voyager II 43

West Germany 21